The Berenstain Bears®
Christmas Fun

Sticker & Activity Book

Copyright © 2016 by Berenstain Publishing, Inc.
Illustrations © 2016 by Berenstain Publishing, Inc.

ISBN 978-0-310-75384-1
Requests for information should be addressed to:
Zonderkidz, 3900 Sparks Drive SE, Grand Rapids, Michigan 49546

Editor: Mary Hassinger
Interior design: Jody Langely
Cover design: Diane Mielke

Printed in China

16 17 18 19 20 21 /DHC/ 6 5 4 3 2 1

ZONDERkidz

A-Mazing Maze

Brother Bear is helping Mama set up the manger scene for Christmas. But where is the angel? Help Brother find the angel.

Christmas Counting

Count the items in each line. Write how many.

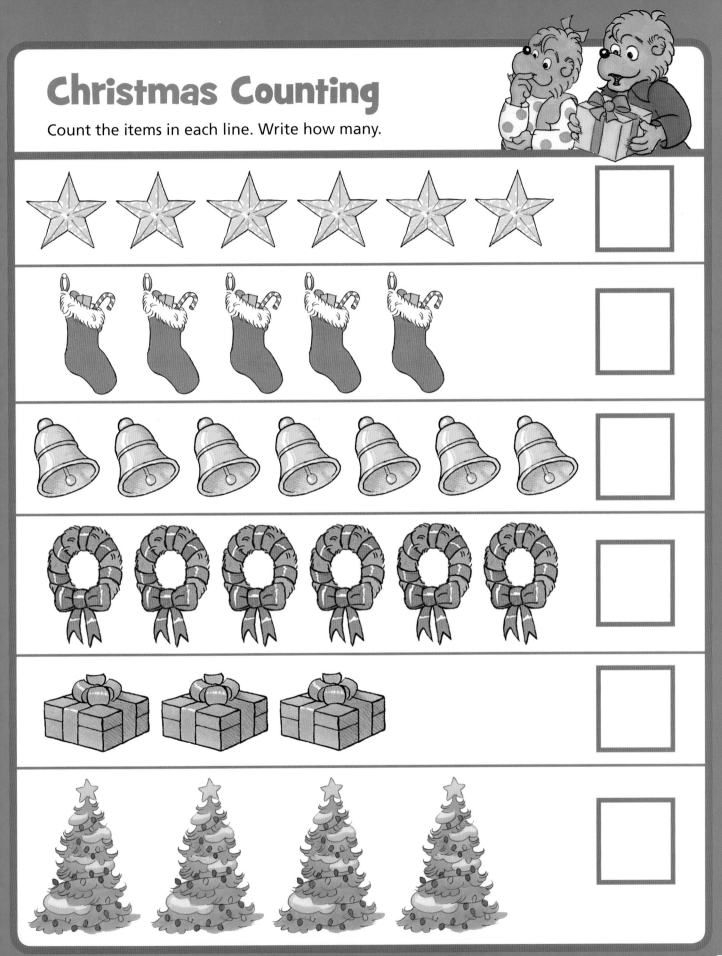

Bear Country Christmas Crossword

Complete the crossword below.

Across
4. Something the Bears decorate
5. His birthday celebration
6. Takes care of sheep
8. Sang to Baby Jesus

Down
1. The wise men brought Jesus these.
2. Where Jesus was born
3. Month of Christmas
6. Animals at the manger
7. Cold white flakes
9. Shines bright in the sky

Christmas Color-by-Number

Look at the Bear family's tree house at Christmastime!
Use the code to color the treehouse.

Color Code

1 =	Yellow	4 =	Blue
2 =	Green	5 =	Brown
3 =	Red	6 =	Purple

Make a Match

Christmas is a time for love. Who takes care of and loves each other?
Draw a line to match them.

Listen to the Angel!

An angel of the Lord appeared to shepherds in the field. The angel had a very important message for them.

Use the code below to find out what the angel said to the shepherds.

Decoder

1	2	3	4	5	6	7	8	9	10	11	12	13
A	B	C	D	E	F	G	H	I	J	K	L	M

14	15	16	17	18	19	20	21	22	23	24	25	26
N	O	P	Q	R	S	T	U	V	W	X	Y	Z

The angel said, ___ ___   ___ ___ ___   ___ ___
            4   15   14   15   20   2   5

___ ___ ___ ___ ___ ___ .   I bring you good news that
1   6   18   1   9   4

will cause great joy for all the people.   Today in the town of David

___ ___ ___ ___ ___ ___
1   19   1   22   9   15   18

has been ___ ___ ___ ___ to you.
            2   15   18   14

A Trip Home

Joseph and Mary had to go to Bethlehem. That is where Joseph's family was from. It was a long trip, and Mary was close to having her baby.

Mary and Joseph saw many things on the way to Bethlehem. Circle 10 things they would not have seen.

Find these objects in the picture.

Baby Jesus

Jesus was born in a stable with animals all around.
Use stickers to finish the picture. Then color.

A Christmas Tree to Remember

Help the Bear family decorate their Christmas tree. Use stickers to help. Can you put the star on top?

We Love Christmas Treats

Honey Bear loves pumpkin pie. Mama Bear made one for Christmas dinner. Help Honey find the pie.

Let's Visit Baby Jesus

The shepherds are happy. They get to see baby Jesus. Just like the angel said, he is with Mary and Joseph in a manger. Color the picture below.

Happy Birthday, Jesus

Find the words in the word search. Circle them.
Use the word bank.

```
E B N A A Z B G I F T S U C P S H U D K
D S K A H S M J P I A A A N S A T R E E
D Y S T D A P I I V S S A Q H E J H N D
K I V T N X U K I B H G H P E A J O Y I
E Z I G G L I O V Z E P Q M P C A M E L
K L E G N A R W O M E Y W I H P Y M P Z
Q R E R E J E S U S P J D R E G Y X H V
U M M A P V M E O V E X I M R J Q W T F
N D H R R I I J N E L S X M D D Y U Y W
U K O A M M R L R C T Z I R M Z F Q O X
K V N N H M F E W M F H G F X G A B I M
K H H Z K G H U A E D N C D I V O L P P
Z G R T Q E X S K H S D S M U J G P J W
Z O K B T Y Y Y K E N S H S S S U I B J
Y L S G S A B V S L A O N T V B B I X N
H U C T B U N A O H V U R A A L E X L Z
V U M N D N U U B T M M A R Y X V C Y G
J B G I G D N P K E W B I E L A M L T I
D C U C V P I V J B H X N A A A U D Y P
I X D J B U N S L T B L V N J B B N T C
```

Word Bank

ANGEL	BABY	BETHLEHEM	CAMEL
CHRISTMAS	DONKEY	GIFTS	JESUS
JOSEPH	MANGER	MARY	SAVIOR
SHEEP	SHEPHERD	STAR	TREE

15

Home, Sweet Home

Learn how to draw the Bear family's tree house. Trace the dotted line to outline the right half of the picture. Use the door and window stickers to help. Draw and color wintery details.

Riding on Camels

The wise men came from the east. They were riding camels.
Connect the dots to draw the camels. Color the picture.

A Party for Jesus!

Jesus was a very special baby. Many people came to visit him. They showed him how much he was loved.

Finish this picture. Read and follow the directions. Then use stickers and crayons or coloring pencils.

1. Color the camel brown.

2. Draw 5 more stars in the sky.

3. Draw a sheep next to Mary.

4. Write "Happy Birthday, Jesus!" across the top of the page.

Who Else Came?

There were animals in the stable where Jesus was born.
How many animals saw baby Jesus on Christmas Day?

doves

mice

cats

sheep

camels

Winter Fun Word Search

Find the words in the word search.
Circle them. Use the word bank.

```
S Q D H M O L Q Y B S F O P D
J E D I D K I G K M L R Y A K
R M K L C Z G L A R I E D V G
K E O A W I E I E M P E A X H
C C T B L V C B G S P Z Z V J
Z D U N O F M L N S E E R M U
S S C H I E W O E G R R U V Y
A A S B C W W O I B Y I C E T
M F O E L M X S N E T T I M S
T A D C A I C E K S T O O B O
S Z E N O A Z D R I F T S Z R
I N K D R C Q Z E W K W Z V F
R E G F Q S D O A Z S O A I R
H C X U C O O I N R N N H J Z
C S L E D D I N G W D S L N U
```

Word Bank

BLIZZARD
BOOTS
CHRISTMAS
COCOA
COLD
DECEMBER
DRIFTS
FREEZE
FROSTY
ICE
ICICLE
MITTENS
SCARF
SHOVEL
SLEDDING
SLIPPERY
SNOW
SNOWFLAKES
SNOWMAN
WINTER

The Joy of Giving

Can you spot the differences between the two pictures?
There are six. Circle them.

Three of a Kind?

Look at each row. Two are the same. One is different. Put an X on the one that is different.

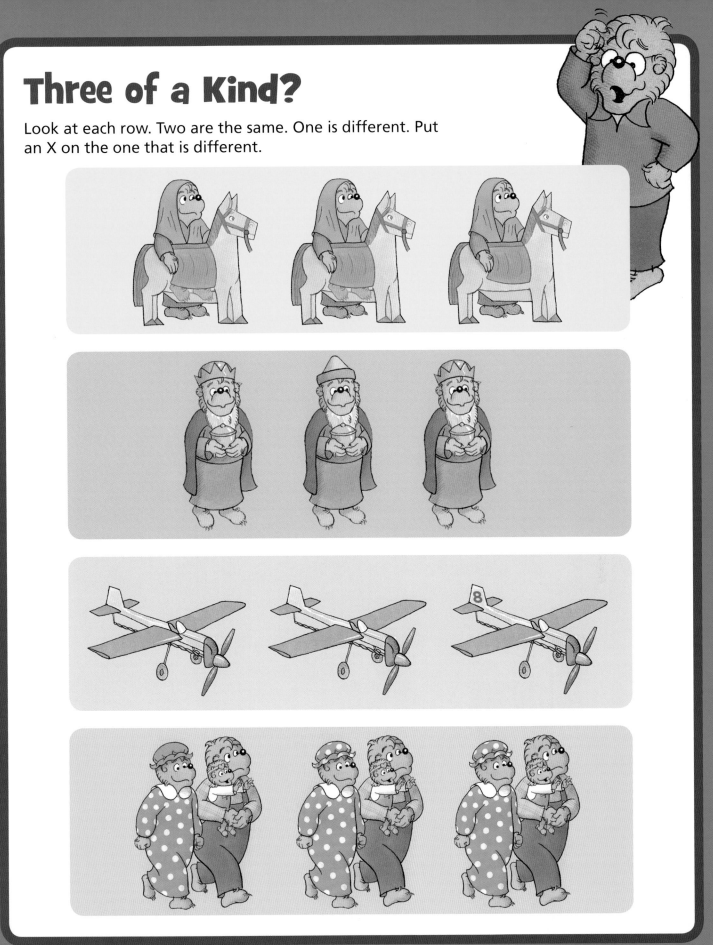

Bear Country Winter Wonderland

Brother, Sister, and Honey are ready for wintertime fun!
Color the tree house. Use stickers to help finish the fun.

Wintertime Patterns

Look at each pattern. Decide which item comes next.
Use a sticker to complete the pattern.

Fill It In

Fill in the blanks. Use the word bank for help.

1. We celebrate Jesus' birthday on _____.

2. The _____ brought the good news of Jesus' birth to the shepherds.

3. Sometimes people put a _____ on top of their Christmas tree like the one that shined bright on Christmas Eve.

4. _____ is the mother of baby Jesus.

5. Jesus was born in the town of _____.

6. _____ wise men brought gifts to Jesus after he was born.

7. The wise men brought Jesus gifts of _____, frankincense, and myrrh.

8. The angels sang, "Glory to God! _____ on earth!"

Word Bank

Bethlehem	Christmas
Star	Gold
Mary	Angels
Peace	Three

Sing a Christmas Song

The Bear family is going to sing Christmas songs.
Use the code to help them figure out the words
to Mama's favorite Christmas song.

1	A
2	B
3	C
4	D
5	E
6	F
7	G
8	H
9	I
10	J
11	K
12	L
13	M
14	N
15	O
16	P
17	Q
18	R
19	S
20	T
21	U
22	V
23	W
24	X
25	Y
26	Z

___ ___ ___ ___ ___ ___
19   9   12   5   14   20

___ ___ ___ ___ ___
14   9   7   8   20

___ ___ ___ ___   night.
8   15   12   25

___ ___ ___ ___ ___   calm.
1   12   12   9   19

All is ___ ___ ___ ___ ___ ___ .
2   18   9   7   8   20

28

Cheering for a Snowy Christmas

Brother, Sister, and Honey love the snow.
Color the picture. Use stickers to help finish it.

Snow Starts with 'S'

The Bear cubs love the snow. The word snow begins with the letter S.
Circle the other things on this page that begin with the letter S.
Write an S next to each picture that has S as the first sound.

Star

Bunny

Sun

Skate

BrotherBear

Stamp

Stocking

Bell

Write the letter S on the line below.

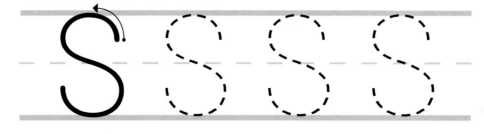

Christmas Tree Trail

Help Papa Bear find the best Christmas tree. Trace the path. Use a red crayon. Color the rest of the tree green.

Post It! Color this Christmas greeting. Hang it on the door. Use stickers to finish it.

Merry Christmas!